This is Liz. She has a skill.

I can go dull. I am hidden!

Tish and Tash check …

No cops!

Liz is hidden.

Tish and Tash go to rob the choc shop.

I can unlock it!

Choc Shop

Click! Click!

Tish and Tash smell the chocs.

choc

mint

milk

Sniff!

Mmmm!

But then Liz rings the cops.

Be quick!